Books by Jon Winokur

A Curmudgeon's Garden of Love

Advice to Writers

Encyclopedia Neurotica

Fathers

Friendly Advice

Happy Motoring (with Norrie Epstein)

How to Win at Golf Without Actually Playing Well

Je Ne Sais What?

Mondo Canine

The Portable Curmudgeon

The Portable Curmudgeon Redux

The Rich Are Different

The Traveling Curmudgeon

True Confessions

The War Between the State

Writers on Writing

Zen to Go

In Passing

Condolences *and* Complaints
ON Death, Dying,
and Related Disappointments

Jon Winokur

SASQUATCH BOOKS
SEATTLE

©2005 by Jon Winokur

Printed in Canada
Published by Sasquatch Books
Distributed by Publishers Group West
10 09 08 07 06 05   8 7 6 5 4 3 2 1

Book design: Kate Basart
Copy editor: Julie Van Pelt

Library of Congress Cataloging-in-Publication Data
In passing : condolences and complaints on death, dying, and related
disappointments / collected by Jon Winokur.
          p.   cm.
ISBN 1-57061-445-8
1. Death--Quotations, maxims, etc. I. Winokur, Jon.

PN6084.D4I5 2005
306.9--dc22

                              2004051375

Sasquatch Books
119 South Main Street, Suite 400
Seattle, WA 98104
206/467-4300
www.sasquatchbooks.com
custserv@sasquatchbooks.com

Patch grief with proverbs.

— William Shakespeare

Introduction

Death, of course, has been a preoccupation for every culture, and in these pages I've tried to collect a wide range of commentary about death from a wide variety of sources, from the Bible to Yogi Berra, from Plato and Socrates to Sigmund Freud and *The Simpsons*.

Over the centuries death has had many names: the "grim reaper," the "last roundup," the "final curtain," "Pale Death." And many faces: death is a "delightful journey," an "escape mechanism," a "faithful companion," even a "democracy" (i.e., "we're all cremated equal" in the "republic of the grave"). Death is "the sound of distant thunder at a picnic." Death "comes like a gas bill that one can't pay." Death is a "great surprise," a "natural appointment," a "warfare accomplished," "the final awakening," and "the golden key to the palace of eternity."

There are observations about death that may or may not be obvious: Death is "the sine qua non of immortality." Death is "the cure of all diseases." Death is "going over to the majority." Death is "part of life" (yeah, the last part). Death is the end, of course, but it's also "a beginning." And have you noticed that "everybody wants to go to heaven but nobody wants to die"?

Here, then, are expressions of fear, anger, denial, fascination, awe, and acceptance in the face of death. What can we glean from these pearls of morbid wisdom? If there's a bottom line, maybe it's that death is the ultimate common denominator, the supreme fact of life that gives meaning to our brief existence and finally makes it precious. Or maybe life and death have no meaning at all. In any case let us not procrastinate, because one thing is clear: we're all just passing through.

— *J. W., Pacific Palisades*

Dust thou art, and unto dust shalt thou return.

— *Genesis 3:19*

✠

Must not all things at the last be swallowed up in death?

— *Plato*

✠

If we may assume as an experience admitting of no exception that every living thing dies from causes within itself, and returns to the inorganic, we can only say, "The goal of all life is death."

— *Sigmund Freud*

Death is a low chemical trick played on
everybody except sequoia trees.

— *J. J. Furnas*

✠

Death: going over to the majority.

— *Thomas Carlyle*

✠

To stop sinning suddenly.

— *Elbert Hubbard*

Death is the sound of distant thunder at a picnic.

— *W. H. Auden*

✠

Death is the messiah. That's the real truth.

— *Isaac Bashevis Singer*

✠

Death is as casual—and often as unexpected—as birth.

— *Jim Bishop*

Death borders upon our birth, and our cradle stands in the grave. Our birth is nothing but our death begun.

— *Bishop Hall*

✝

Life is pleasant. Death is peaceful. It's the transition that's troublesome.

— *Isaac Asimov*

✝

The Five Stages of Dying: denial, anger, bargaining, depression, and acceptance.

— *Elisabeth Kübler-Ross*

Death is the greatest evil, because it cuts off hope.

    — William Hazlitt

    ✝

On the plus side, death is one of the few things that can be done just as easily lying down.

    — Woody Allen

    ✝

Only music can speak of death.

    — André Malraux

Death is psychosomatic.

— Charles Manson

✢

When Kleinzeit opened the door of his flat
Death was there, black and hairy and ugly,
no bigger than a medium-sized chimpanzee
with dirty fingernails.

— Russell Hoban

Death is simply a shedding of the physical body, like the butterfly coming out of a cocoon. It's like putting away your winter coat when spring comes.

— *Elisabeth Kübler-Ross*

✝

Death used to announce itself in the thick of life but now people drag on so long it sometimes seems that we are reaching the stage when we may have to announce ourselves to death. . . . It is as though one needs a special strength to die, and not a final weakness.

— *Ronald Blythe*

Death is the only thing we haven't
succeeded in completely vulgarizing.

—*Aldous Huxley*

✠

The reports of my death have been greatly
exaggerated.

—*Mark Twain*

✠

The best of men cannot suspend their fate:
The good die early, and the bad die late.

—*Daniel Defoe*

"After she was dead I loved her." That is the story of every life—and death.

— Gore Vidal

✝

. . . Then worms shall try
That long preserved virginity,
And your quaint honor turn to dust,
And into ashes all my lust.
The grave's a fine and private place,
But none, I think, do there embrace.

— Andrew Marvell

There will be sex after death. We just won't be able to feel it.

— *Lily Tomlin*

✝

The difference between sex and death is that with death you can do it alone and no one is going to make fun of you.

— *Woody Allen*

✝

Whenever I prepare for a journey I prepare as for death. Should I never return, all is in order. This is what life has taught me.

— *Katherine Mansfield*

Death is both a threat and a promise.

— *Howard Ogden*

✝

Death, old captain, it is time, let us raise the anchor!

— *Charles Baudelaire*

✝

Let 'er R.I.P.

— *The Simpsons*

We die, and we do not die.

— Zen saying

✠

I'd hate to die twice. It's so boring.

— Richard Feynman (last words)

✠

Even in the valley of the shadow of death,
two and two do not make six.

*— Leo Tolstoy (refusing deathbed conversion to the
Russian Orthodox Church)*

Most people die at the last minute, others twenty years beforehand, some even earlier. They are the wretched of the earth.

— Louis-Ferdinand Céline

✠

No one can die now without teddy bears and candles being left at a fence.

— George Carlin

✠

Death may be the greatest of all human blessings.

— Socrates

13

Sleep is good, death is better; but the best thing would be never to have been born at all.

— *Heinrich Heine*

✝

When a man lies dying, he does not die from disease alone. He dies from his whole life.

— *Charles Péguy*

✝

It's funny the way most people love the dead. Once you're dead, you're made for life.

— *Jimi Hendrix*

14

Goddammit! He beat me to it.

— Janis Joplin (on hearing of Jimi Hendrix's death)

✛

I'm not afraid of life and I'm not afraid of death: dying's the bore.

— Katherine Anne Porter

As the poets have mournfully sung,
Death takes the innocent young,
The rolling-in-money,
The screamingly funny,
And those who are very well hung.

— *W. H. Auden*

✝

Modern thought has transferred the spectral
character of Death to the notion of time
itself. Time has become Death triumphant
over all.

— *John Berger*

There are more dead people than living, and their numbers are increasing.

— *Eugene Ionesco*

✝

If I had any decency, I'd be dead. Most of my friends are.

— *Dorothy Parker (at age seventy)*

✝

Being over seventy is like being engaged in a war. All our friends are going or gone and we survive amongst the dead and the dying as on a battlefield.

— *Muriel Spark*

I cannot forgive my friends for dying; I do not find these vanishing acts of theirs at all amusing.

— Logan Pearsall Smith

✠

Each departed friend is a magnet that attracts us to the next world.

— Jean Paul Richter

✠

While we are mourning the loss of our friend, others are rejoicing to meet him behind the veil.

— John Taylor

On a day of burial there is no perspective—
for space itself is annihilated. Your dead
friend is still a fragmentary being. The day
you bury him is a day of chores and crowds,
of hands false or true to be shaken, of the
immediate cares of mourning. The dead
friend will not really die until tomorrow,
when silence is round you again. Then he
will show himself complete, as he was—to
tear himself away, as he was, from the
substantial you. Only then will you cry out
because of him who is leaving and whom
you cannot detain.

—Antoine de Saint-Exupéry

I have lost friends, some by death, others through sheer inability to cross the street.

—*Virginia Woolf*

✠

Death ends a life, not a relationship.

—*Morrie Schwartz*

✠

As men, we are all equal in the presence of death.

—*Publilius Syrus*

Pale Death with impartial tread beats at the poor man's cottage door and at the palaces of kings.

— Horace

✛

In the democracy of the dead all men at last are equal. There is neither rank nor station nor prerogative in the republic of the grave.

— John J. Ingalls

✛

We're all cremated equal.

— Goodman Ace

Horror at the sight of death turns into
satisfaction that it is someone else who is
dead.

— *Elias Canetti*

✛

Is there a reasonable person who at a
significant moment does not deep in his soul
think of anything but death?

— *Arthur Schnitzler*

✛

Everybody knows everybody is dying. That's
why people are as good as they are.

— *Mark Harris*

Men have a much better time of it than women. For one thing, they marry later, for another thing, they die earlier.

— H. L. Mencken

✦

Dying is no big deal. The least of us will manage that. Living is the trick.

— Red Smith

✦

There's no bad mother, and no good death.

— Yiddish proverb

Death comes along like a gas bill one can't pay—and that's all one can say about it.

— *Anthony Burgess*

✢

I refuse to let death hamper life. Death must enter life only to define it.

— *Jean-Paul Sartre*

✢

Everybody has got to die, but I always believed an exception would be made in my case. Now what?

— *William Saroyan (a few hours before his death)*

Mortality is not simply an avoidable accident, but a natural appointment, from which there is no hope of escape.

— *Jonathan Miller*

✠

The greatest dignity to be found in death is the dignity of the life that preceded it. Hope resides in the meaning of what our lives have been.

— *Sherwin B. Nuland*

Of all escape mechanisms, death is the most efficient.

— H. L. Mencken

✛

Life is a great surprise. I do not see why death should not be an even greater one.

— Vladimir Nabokov

✛

Death is part of life. The last part.

— Anonymous

Death is a faithful companion of life and follows it like its shadow.

— *Carl Jung*

✝

The irony of man's condition is that the deepest need is to be free of the anxiety of death and annihilation; but it is life itself which awakens it, and so we must shrink from being fully alive.

— *Ernest Becker*

Courage is almost a contradiction in terms. It means a strong will to live taking the form of a readiness to die.

— *G. K. Chesterton*

✦

Watching a peaceful death of a human being reminds us of a falling star; one of a million lights in a vast sky that flares up for a brief moment only to disappear into the endless night forever.

— *Elisabeth Kübler-Ross*

Mendacity is a system that we live in. Liquor is one way out, and death's the other.

— *Tennessee Williams*

✢

Man is the only animal that finds his own existence a problem he has to solve, and from which he cannot escape. In the same sense man is the only animal who knows he must die.

— *Erich Fromm*

Death is nature's way of telling us to slow down.

— Anonymous

✠

The human animal dances wildest on the edge of the grave.

— Rita Mae Brown

✠

Death tugs at my ears and says: live, for I am coming.

— Oliver Wendell Holmes

One thing is certain and the rest is lies:
the flower that once has bloomed forever
dies.

   — *Edward Fitzgerald*

✛

Neither in the hearts of men nor in the
manners of society will there be a lasting
peace until we outlaw death.

   — *Albert Camus*

✛

That it will never come again
Is what makes life so sweet.

   — *Emily Dickinson*

Since the day of my birth, my death began its walk. It is walking toward me, without hurrying.

— *Jean Cocteau*

✠

Death is the absence of life . . . there is no evil in it.

— *M. R. Cohen*

✠

Men fear death, as children fear to go in the dark; and as that natural fear in children is increased with tales, so is the other.

— *Francis Bacon*

The fear of death is more to be dreaded than death itself.

— *Publilius Syrus*

✟

I adore life but I don't fear death. I just prefer to die as late as possible.

— *Georges Simenon*

✟

Tired of living,
And scared of dying.

— *Oscar Hammerstein II, "Ol' Man River"*

Death has but one terror—that it has no
tomorrow.

      — Eric Hoffer

    ✝

The fear of death is the most unjustified of
all fears, for there's no risk of accident to
someone who's dead.

      — Albert Einstein

Death be not proud, though some have
    called thee
Mighty and dreadful, for thou art not so.
For those whom thou think'st thou dost
    overthrow
Die not, poor Death, nor yet canst thou
    kill me.

— John Donne

✠

I don't believe in dying. It's been done.

— George Burns

The dead know only one thing: it is better to be alive.

— *James Elroy Flecker*

✠

I'm so happy dancing while the grim reaper cuts, cuts, cuts, but he can't get me. I'm as clever as can be, and I'm very quick but don't forget; we've only got so many tricks. No one lives forever.

— *Danny Elfman*

Because I could not stop for Death,
He kindly stopped for me—
The Carriage held but just Ourselves
And Immortality.

— Emily Dickinson

✛

The first requisite for immortality is death.

— Stanislaw J. Lec

✛

I think immortality is an overrated
commodity.

— S. N. Behrman

I don't want to achieve immortality through my work, I want to achieve it by not dying.

— *Woody Allen*

✠

If I have any beliefs about immortality, it is that certain dogs I have known will go to heaven, and very, very few persons.

— *James Thurber*

✠

The only thing wrong with immortality is that it tends to go on forever.

— *Herb Caen*

It's incongruous that the older we get, the more likely we are to turn in the direction of religion. Less vivid and intense ourselves, closer to the grave, we begin to conceive of ourselves as immortal.

— *Edward Hoagland*

✝

Death is not an event in life: We do not live to experience death. If we take eternity to mean not infinite temporal duration but timelessness, then eternal life belongs to those who live in the present.

— *Ludwig Wittgenstein*

To himself everyone is an immortal. He may
know that he is going to die, but he can
never know that he is dead.

— Samuel Butler

✛

The survival of personality is neither
conceivable nor desirable.

— Max Nordau

✛

What we have done for ourselves alone dies
with us; what we have done for others and
the world remains and is immortal.

— Albert Pike

Deprived of the hope for immortality,
man ... is the most wretched being on earth.

—Moses Mendelssohn

✠

It must require an inordinate share of
vanity and presumption, too, after enjoying
so much that is good and beautiful on earth,
to ask the Lord for immortality in addition
to it all.

—Heinrich Heine

Millions long for immortality who do not know what to do with themselves on a rainy Sunday afternoon.

— Susan Ertz

✠

He had decided to live forever or die in the attempt.

— Joseph Heller

Because men really respect only that which was founded of old and has developed slowly, he who wants to live on after his death must take care not only of his posterity but even more of his past.

— *Nietzsche*

✝

The flattery of posterity is not worth much more than contemporary flattery, which is worth nothing.

— *Jorge Luis Borges*

Posterity gives every man his true value.

— Publius Cornelius Tacitus

✛

Posterity is as likely to be wrong as anybody else.

— Heywood Broun

✛

Posterity is just around the corner.

— George S. Kaufman

The only thing you take with you when you're gone is what you leave behind.

— *John Allston*

✦

When I die, I die. I have never believed in personal survival. An eternity of G.B.S. or anyone else is unthinkable. Individuals perish, but creation goes on. I believe in Life Everlasting, not in Smith, Brown, Jones and Robinson everlasting.

— *George Bernard Shaw*

We never become really and genuinely our entire and honest selves until we are dead— and not then until we have been dead years and years. People ought to start dead and then they would be honest so much earlier.

— Mark Twain

✦

The graveyards are full of indispensable people.

— Charles de Gaulle

Far from being irreplaceable, we should be replaced. Fantasies of staying the hand of mortality are incompatible with the best interests of our species and the continuity of humankind's progress.

— Sherwin B. Nuland

✠

A single death is a tragedy; a million deaths is a statistic.

— Joseph Stalin

How could they tell?

— Dorothy Parker (informed that Calvin Coolidge had died)

✠

Working through our endings allows us to redefine our relationships, to surrender what is dead and to accept what is alive, and to be in the world more fully to face the new situation.

— Stanley Keleman

Time rushes towards us with its hospital tray
of infinitely varied narcotics, even while
it is preparing us for its inevitably fatal
operation.

— *Tennessee Williams*

✛

Perhaps the gods are kind to us by making
life more disagreeable as we grow older. In
the end, death seems less intolerable than
the manifold burdens we carry.

— *Sigmund Freud*

We're all paid off in the end, and the fools first.

— *Tallulah Bankhead*

✝

Better a noble death than a wretched life.

— *Yiddish proverb*

✝

Whoever has lived long enough to find out what life is, knows how deep a debt of gratitude we owe to Adam, the first great benefactor of our race. He brought death into the world.

— *Mark Twain*

Many times man lives and dies
Between his two eternities.

— William Butler Yeats

✠

Men talk of killing time, while time quietly
kills them.

— Dion Boucicault

✠

As if you could kill time without injuring
eternity.

— Henry David Thoreau

Life is hardly more than a fraction of a second. Such a little time to prepare oneself for eternity!

— *Paul Gauguin*

✠

Death is a commingling of eternity with time; in the death of a good man, eternity is seen looking through time.

— *Goethe*

✠

Death is no more than a turning of us over from time to eternity.

— *William Penn*

All that live must die, passing through nature to eternity.

— *William Shakespeare*

✝

Death is the golden key that opens the palace of eternity.

— *John Milton*

✝

Rest, rest, shall I have not all eternity to rest?

— *Antoine Arnauld*

Eternity's a terrible thought. I mean, where's it all going to end?

— *Tom Stoppard*

In days gone by, we were afraid of dying in dishonor or a state of sin. Nowadays, we are afraid of dying fools. Now the fact is that there is no Extreme Unction to absolve us of foolishness. We endure it here on earth as subjective eternity.

— *Jean Baudrillard*

Nothing in life is certain except death and taxes.

— Benjamin Franklin

✠

There will always be death and taxes; however, death doesn't get worse every year.

— Anonymous

✠

Death and taxes and childbirth! There's never any convenient time for any of them.

— Margaret Mitchell

There is no goal better than this one: to know as you lie on your deathbed that you lived your true life, and you did whatever made you happy.

— *Steve Chandler*

✦

For what is it to die,
But to stand in the sun and melt into the
    wind?
And when the Earth has claimed our limbs,
Then we shall truly dance.

— *Kahlil Gibran*

The day which we fear as our last is but the birthday of eternity.

— Seneca

✦

Death is not extinguishing the light;
it is putting out the lamp because dawn
has come.

— Rabindranath Tagore

✦

If a man hasn't discovered something that
he will die for, he isn't fit to live.

— Martin Luther King, Jr.

He is one of those people who would be
enormously improved by death.

    — H. H. Munroe

    ✛

I didn't attend the funeral, but I sent a nice
letter saying I approved of it.

    — Mark Twain

    ✛

I have never killed a man, but I have read
many obituaries with great pleasure.

    — Clarence Darrow

Some men are alive simply because it is against the law to kill them.

— Ed Howe

✠

Nobody owns life, but anyone who can pick up a frying pan owns death.

— William S. Burroughs

When I look back on all these worries, I remember the story of the old man who said on his deathbed that he had had a lot of trouble in his life, most of which had never happened.

— *Winston Churchill*

✦

Death is the cure of all diseases.

— *Anonymous*

To be idle is a short road to death and to be diligent is a way of life; foolish people are idle, wise people are diligent.

—*Buddha*

✠

Every man dies. Not every man really lives.

—*William Wallace*

✠

Life is eternal and love is immortal, and death is only a horizon, and a horizon is nothing save the limit of our sight.

—*Rossiter W. Raymond*

A man is not completely born until he is dead.

— *Benjamin Franklin*

✛

Nothing can happen more beautiful than death.

— *Walt Whitman*

✛

Death is the most beautiful adventure in life.

— *Charles Frohman*

Do not go gentle into that good night,
Old age should burn and rage at close
of day;
Rage, rage against the dying of the light.

—*Dylan Thomas*

✠

Death is no different whined at than
withstood.

—*Philip Larkin*

What we commonly call death does not destroy the body, it only causes a separation of spirit and body.

— Brigham Young

✛

Be of good cheer about death and know this as a truth—that no evil can happen to a good man, either in life or after death.

— Socrates

✛

Is death the last sleep? No, it is the last and final awakening.

— Sir Walter Scott

Many men on the point of an edifying death would be furious if they were suddenly restored to health.

— *Cesare Pavese*

✝

We sometimes congratulate ourselves at the moment of waking from a troubled dream . . . it may be so at the moment of death.

— *Nathaniel Hawthorne*

✝

Birth and Death are the two noblest expressions of bravery.

— *Kahlil Gibran*

I shall not die of a cold. I shall die of having lived.

— Willa Cather

✦

Death is when you get sick one day and you don't get well again. Can't seem to shake it off.

— John Phillips

✦

The difficulty, my friends, is not in avoiding death, but in avoiding unrighteousness, for that runs faster than death.

— Socrates

It is foolish to be afraid of death. JUST THINK!!
No more repaired tires on the body vehicle,
no more patchwork living.

— *Paramhansa Yogananda*

✛

I would rather live and love where death is
king than have eternal life where love is not.

— *Robert G. Ingersoll*

✛

To infinite, ever present Love, all is Love,
and there is no error, no sin, sickness, nor
death.

— *Mary Baker Eddy*

Without an understanding of myth or
religion, without an understanding of
the relationship between destruction and
creation, death and rebirth, the individual
suffers the mysteries of life as meaningless
mayhem alone.

— Marion Woodman

✠

For life in the present there is no death.
Death is not an event in life. It is not a fact
in the world.

— Ludwig Wittgenstein

Because I have loved life, I shall have no sorrow to die.

— *Amelia Burr*

✛

Our fear of death is like our fear that summer will be short, but when we have had our swing of pleasure, our fill of fruit, and our swelter of heat, we say we have had our day.

— *Ralph Waldo Emerson*

Even death is not to be feared by one who
has lived wisely.

—*Buddha*

✤

Death? Why this fuss about death. Use
your imagination, try to visualize a world
without death! Death is the essential
condition of life, not an evil.

—*Charlotte Perkins Gilman*

The idea of death, the fear of it, haunts
the human animal like nothing else; it is
a mainspring of human activity—designed
largely to avoid the fatality of death, to
overcome it by denying in some way that
it is the final destiny of man.

— *Ernest Becker*

Down, down, down into the darkness of the
    grave
Gently they go, the beautiful, the tender,
    the kind;
Quietly they go, the intelligent, the witty,
    the brave.
I know. But I do not approve. And I am not
    resigned.

Edna St. Vincent Millay

Religion is the human response to being
alive and having to die.

F. Forrester Church

I wanted a perfect ending. Now I've learned, the hard way, that some poems don't rhyme, and some stories don't have a clear beginning, middle, and end. Life is about not knowing, having to change, taking the moment and making the best of it, without knowing what's going to happen next. Delicious ambiguity.

— Gilda Radner

Tell me not, in mournful numbers,
Life is but an empty dream!
For the soul is dead that slumbers,
and things are not what they seem.
Life is real! Life is earnest!
And the grave is not its goal;
Dust thou art; to dust returnest,
Was not spoken of the soul.

— Henry Wadsworth Longfellow

✝

If my doctor told me I had only six minutes
to live, I wouldn't brood. I'd type a little
faster.

— Isaac Asimov

Too many people are thinking of security instead of opportunity. They seem to be more afraid of life than death.

James F. Byrnes

✠

Beth could not reason upon or explain the faith that gave her courage and patience to give up life, and cheerfully wait for death. Like a confiding child, she asked no questions, but left everything to God and nature, Father and Mother of us all, feeling sure that they, and they only, could teach and strengthen heart and spirit for this life and the life to come.

Louisa May Alcott

When we finally know we are dying, and
all other sentient beings are dying with
us, we start to have a burning, almost
heartbreaking sense of the fragility and
preciousness of each moment and each
being, and from this can grow a deep, clear,
limitless compassion for all beings.

— *Sogyal Rinpoche*

✝

There's no need to get out of bed for it;
Wherever you may be,
They bring it to you free.

— *Kingsley Amis*

I want to die young at an advanced age.

— *Max Lerner*

✝

What I look forward to is continued
immaturity followed by death.

— *Dave Barry*

Why do we have to die? As a kid you get
nice little white shoes with white laces and a
velvet suit with short pants and a nice collar
and you go to college, you meet a nice girl
and get married, work a few years and then
you have to *die*! What is that shit? They
never wrote that in the contract!

— *Mel Brooks*

✠

Now if the harvest is over
And the world cold
Give me the bonus of laughter
As I lose hold.

— *John Betjeman*

There are worse things in life than death.
Have you ever spent an evening with an
insurance salesman?

— Woody Allen

✛

In a way dying is like having children—
you never know what will come out.

— Joseph Heller

✛

Life is not lost by dying; life is lost minute
by minute, day by dragging day, in all the
thousand small uncaring ways.

— Stephen Vincent Benét

He who dies a thousand deaths meets the final hour with the calmness of one who approaches a well remembered door.

— Heywood Broun

I look upon life as a gift from God. I did nothing to earn it. Now that the time is coming to give it back, I have no right to complain.

— Joyce Cary

Death is not the greatest loss in life. The greatest loss is what dies inside us while we live.

— *Norman Cousins*

✝

Our life is made by the death of others.

— *Leonardo da Vinci*

Science says: "We must live," and seeks the means of prolonging, increasing, facilitating and amplifying life, of making it tolerable and acceptable. Wisdom says: "We must die," and seeks how to make us die well.

— *Miguel de Unamuno*

✝

Death is not so serious. Pain is.

— *André Malraux*

What greater pain could mortals have than this: to see their children dead before their eyes?

— Euripedes

✣

How frighteningly few are the persons whose death would spoil our appetite and make the world seem empty.

— Eric Hoffer

✣

'Tis after death that we measure men.

— James Barron Hope

A man's dying is more the survivors' affair than his own.

— Thomas Mann

✠

Death teaches us to live; it gives us a boundary to map our living within. Death's hammer breaks through the mirror separating us from light.

— David Meltzer

✠

People living deeply have no fear of death.

— Anaïs Nin

Men fear death, as if unquestionably the greatest evil, and yet no man knows that it may not be the greatest good.

— *William Mitford*

✠

One wants to stay alive, of course, but one only stays alive by virtue of the fear of death.

— *George Orwell*

✠

Some people are so afraid to die that they never begin to live.

— *Henry Van Dyke*

It's not that I'm afraid to die, I just don't want to be there when it happens.

— Woody Allen

✠

Life is a sickness which sleep relieves every sixteen hours; but it is only a palliative. Death is the remedy.

— Nicolas Chamfort

✠

The display of grief makes more demands than grief itself. How few men are sad in their own company.

— Seneca

Bereavement is a darkness impenetrable to the imagination of the unbereaved.

— Iris Murdoch

✟

Nothing becomes so offensive so quickly as grief. When fresh it finds someone to console it, but when it becomes chronic, it is ridiculed, and rightly.

— Seneca

While grief is fresh, every attempt to divert
only irritates. You must wait till grief be
digested, and then amusement will dissipate
the remains of it.

— *Samuel Johnson*

The memory of most men is an abandoned
cemetery where lie, unsung and unhonored,
the dead whom they have ceased to cherish.
Any lasting grief is reproof to their
forgetfulness.

— *Marguerite Yourcenar*

Grief can take care of itself, but to get the full value of a joy you must have somebody to divide it with.

— *Mark Twain*

Early to rise and early to bed
Makes a male healthy, wealthy and dead.

— *James Thurber*

I'm not going to die, I'm going home like a shooting star.

— *Sojourner Truth*

All say "How hard it is that we have to die"—a strange complaint to come from the mouths of people who have had to live.

— Mark Twain

Is there not a certain satisfaction in the fact that natural limits are set to the life of the individual, so that at its conclusion it may appear as a work of art?

— Albert Einstein

Cemetery, *n.* An isolated suburban spot where mourners match lies, poets write at a target and stone-cutters spell for a wager.

— *Ambrose Bierce*

✝

Boy, when you're dead they really fix you up. I hope to hell when I *do* die somebody has sense enough to dump me in the river or something. Anything except sticking me in a goddam cemetery. People coming and putting a bunch of flowers on your stomach on Sunday, and all that crap. Who wants flowers when you're dead? Nobody.

— *J. D. Salinger*

The guilt of the quick raises monuments to the dead.

— Allan Wheelis

✠

Grave, *n.* A place in which the dead are laid to await the coming of the medical student.

— Ambrose Bierce

✠

Do not stand at my grave and weep; I am not there. I do not sleep. I am a thousand winds that blow. I am the diamond glints on snow.

— Clare Harner Lyon

Epitaph, *n.* An inscription on a tomb, showing that virtues acquired by death have a retroactive effect.

—*Ambrose Bierce*

Epitaph for a dead waiter: God finally caught his eye.

—*George S. Kaufman*

Do not pass by my epitaph, traveler.
But having stopped, listen and learn, then
    go your way.
There is no boat in Hades, no ferryman
    Charon,
No caretaker Aiakos, no dog Cerberus.
All we who are dead below
Have become bones and ashes, but nothing
    else.
I have spoken to you honestly, go on,
    traveler,
Lest even while dead I seem loquacious
    to you.

— Roman epitaph

Tombs are the clothes of the dead and a grave is a plain suit.

— *R. Buckminster Fuller*

✝

An epitaph is a belated advertisement for a line of goods that has been discontinued.

— *Irvin S. Cobb*

✝

The epitaphs on tombstones of a great many people should read: Died at thirty, and buried at sixty.

— *Nicholas Butler*

And were an epitaph to be my story I'd have a short one ready for my own. I would have written of me on my stone: I had a lover's quarrel with the world.

— *Robert Frost*

✦

If men could see the epitaphs their friends write they would believe they had gotten into the wrong grave.

— *American proverb*

Green leaves on a dead tree is our epitaph—
green leaves, dear reader, on a dead tree.

—*Cyril Connolly*

✠

Warm summer sun,
Shine kindly here,
Warm southern wind,
Blow softly here.
Green sod above,
Lie light, lie light.
Good night, dear heart,
Good night, good night.

—*Mark Twain (epitaph for his wife, Olivia)*

Eulogy, *n.* Praise of a person who has either
the advantages of wealth and power, or the
consideration to be dead.

— *Ambrose Bierce*

✠

When we are dead, we are praised by those
who survive us, though we frequently have
no other merit than that of being no longer
alive.

— *La Bruyère*

The dead should be judged like criminals, impartially, but they should be allowed the benefit of the doubt.

— Samuel Butler

✝

The dead cannot cry out for justice; it is a duty of the living to do so for them.

— Lois McMaster Bujold

✝

If you want to really know what your friends and family think of you, die broke, and then see who shows up for the funeral.

— Gregory Nunn

Friends make pretense of following to the
grave but before one is in it, their minds
are turned and making the best of their way
back to life and living people and things
they understand.

— Robert Frost

✠

If you want him to mourn, you had best
leave him nothing.

— Martial

No eulogy is due to him who simply does his duty and nothing more.

— Saint Augustine

What can you say about a twenty-five-year-old girl who died? That she was beautiful? And brilliant? That she loved Mozart and Bach? And the Beatles? And me?

— Erich Segal

A funeral eulogy is a belated plea for the defense delivered after the evidence is all in.

— Irvin S. Cobb

Of present fame think little, and of future less; the praises that we receive after we are buried, like the flowers that are strewed over our grave, may be gratifying to the living, but they are nothing to the dead.

— *Charles Caleb Colton*

✝

Funeral, *n.* A pageant whereby we attest our respect for the dead by enriching the undertaker, and strengthen our grief by an expenditure that deepens our groans and doubles our tears.

— *Ambrose Bierce*

I hate funerals and would not attend my own if it could be avoided, but it is well for every man to stop once in a while to think of what sort of a collection of mourners he is training for his final event.

— *Robert T. Morris*

✟

Why is it that we rejoice at birth and grieve at a funeral? It is because we are not the person involved.

— *Mark Twain*

The chief mourner does not always attend the funeral.

— Ralph Waldo Emerson

✝

Don't order any black things. Rejoice in his memory, and be radiant: leave grief to the children. Wear violet and purple. . . . Be patient with the poor people who will snivel: they don't know, and they think they will live forever, which makes death a division instead of a bond.

— George Bernard Shaw

Her capacity for family affection is extraordinary. When her third husband died, her hair turned quite gold from grief.

— *Oscar Wilde*

✚

Tears are sometimes an inappropriate response to death. When a life has been lived completely honestly, completely successfully, or just completely, the correct response to death's perfect punctuation mark is a smile.

— *Julie Burchill*

A funeral is not death, any more than baptism is birth or marriage union. All three are the clumsy devices, coming now too late, now too early, by which society would register the quick motions of man.

— *E. M. Forster*

The purpose of a funeral service is to comfort the living. It is important at a funeral to display excessive grief. This will show others how kind-hearted and loving you are and their approved opinion of you will be very comforting.

As anyone familiar with modern fiction and motion pictures knows, excessive grief cannot be expressed by means of tears or a mournful face. It is necessary to break things, hit people, and throw yourself on the top of the coffin, at least.

— *P. J. O'Rourke*

Where a blood relation sobs, an intimate friend should choke up, a distant acquaintance should sigh, a stranger should merely fumble sympathetically with his handkerchief.

— *Mark Twain*

✣

The bitterest tears shed over graves are for words left unsaid and deeds left undone.

— *Harriet Beecher Stowe*

Animals have these advantages over man: they have no theologians to instruct them, their funerals cost them nothing, and no one starts lawsuits over their wills.

— Voltaire

✝

Worldly faces never look so worldly as at a funeral.

They have the same effect of grating incongruity as the sound of a coarse voice breaking the solemn silence of night.

— George Eliot

O death where is thy sting? O grave where is they victory? Where, indeed? Many a badly stung survivor, faced with the aftermath of some relative's funeral, has ruefully conceded that the victory has been won hands down by the funeral establishment—in disastrously unequal battle.

— *Jessica Mitford*

✠

I answer the heroic question "Death, where is thy sting?" with "It is here in my heart and mind and memories."

— *Maya Angelou*

[Funerals are] the cocktail parties of the geriatric set.

— *Harold Macmillan*

✝

A damn good funeral is still one of our best and cheapest acts of theater.

— *Gwyn Thomas*

My grandfather had a wonderful funeral . . .
it was a catered funeral. It was held in a big
hall with accordion players. On the buffet
table there was a replica of the deceased in
potato salad.

— *Woody Allen*

✟

In the city a funeral is just an interruption
of traffic; in the country it is a form of
popular entertainment.

— *George Ade*

You haven't lived until you've died in California.

— *Mort Sahl*

✝

There's nothing like a morning funeral for sharpening the appetite for lunch.

— *Arthur Marshall*

✝

Always go to other people's funerals, otherwise they won't come to yours.

— *Yogi Berra*

They tell me, Lucy, thou art dead,
That all of thee we loved and cherished
Has with thy summer roses perished;
And left, as its young beauty fled,
An ashen memory in its stead.

— *John Greenleaf Whittier*

✝

I think of death as some delightful journey
that I shall take when all my tasks are done.

— *Ella Wheeler Wilcox*

The man that runs away lives to die
another day.

— *A. E. Housman*

✣

It is better to die on your feet than live on
your knees.

— *Emiliano Zapata*

✣

I spend money with reckless abandon. Last
month I blew $5,000 at a reincarnation. I
got to thinking, what the hell, you only live
once!

— *Ronnie Shakes*

I quit flying years ago. I don't want to die with tourists.

— Billy Bob Thornton

✝

If you die in an elevator, be sure to push the Up button.

— Sam Levenson

✝

I don't want to tell you how much insurance I carry with the Prudential, but all I can say is: when I go, they go too.

— Jack Benny

One of the few good things about modern times: If you die horribly on television, you will not have died in vain. You will have entertained us.

— *Kurt Vonnegut*

✠

Death is more universal than life; everyone dies but not everyone lives.

— *A. Sachs*

Even at our birth, death does but stand
aside a little. And every day he looks
towards us and muses somewhat to himself
whether that day or the next he will draw
nigh.

— *Robert Bolt*

✝

Death is better, a milder fate than tyranny.

— *Aeschylus*

✝

Do not fear death so much, but rather the
inadequate life.

— *Bertolt Brecht*

For certain is death for the born
And certain is birth for the dead;
Therefore over the inevitable
Thou shouldst not grieve.

—*Bhagavad Gita*

✛

He not busy being born
Is busy dying.

—*Bob Dylan*

Death, the most dreaded of evils, is of no concern to us; for while we exist death is not present, and when death is present we no longer exist.

— *Epicurus*

✝

Life does not cease to be funny when people die any more than it ceases to be serious when people laugh.

— *George Bernard Shaw*

There is no cure for birth and death save to enjoy the interval.

—George Santayana

✠

For three days after death hair and fingernails continue to grow, but phone calls taper off.

—Johnny Carson

✠

As a well-spent day brings happy sleep, so life well used brings happy death.

—Leonardo da Vinci

Think not disdainfully of death, but look on it with favor; for even death is one of the things that Nature wills.

— Marcus Aurelius

✠

Never knock on Death's door—ring the bell and run away! Death really hates that!

— Matt Frewer (as Dr. Mike Stratford in Doctor, Doctor)

✠

I suppose that I shall have to die beyond my means.

— Oscar Wilde (when told the cost of an operation)

As we look deeply within, we understand our perfect balance. There is no fear of the cycle of birth, life and death. For when you stand in the present moment, you are timeless.

— Rodney Yee

✝

Death is not the worst; rather, in vain
To wish for death, and not to compass it.

— Sophocles

If I could drop dead right now, I'd be the happiest man alive.

— *Samuel Goldwyn*

✠

Death is a very dull, dreary affair, and my advice to you is to have nothing whatever to do with it.

— *W. Somerset Maugham*

✠

Death will be a great relief. No more interviews.

— *Katharine Hepburn*

Dying is a troublesome business: there is pain to be suffered, and it wrings one's heart; but death is a splendid thing— a warfare accomplished, a beginning all over again, a triumph. You can always see that in their faces.

— *George Bernard Shaw*

✛

Those who welcome death have only tried it from the ears up.

— *Wilson Mizner*

The dead govern the living.

— Auguste Comte

✠

The past is all holy to us; the dead are all
holy; even they that were wicked when alive.

— Thomas Carlyle

✠

We owe respect to the living. To the dead we
owe only truth.

— Voltaire

Death doesn't affect the living because it has not happened yet. Death doesn't concern the dead because they have ceased to exist.

— W. Somerset Maugham

✣

De mortuis nil nisi bonum (Say nothing but good of the dead).

— Latin saying

✣

Death is the opening of a more subtle life. In the flower, it sets free the perfume; in the chrysalis, the butterfly; in man, the soul.

— Juliette Adam

It costs me never a stab nor squirm
To tread by chance upon a worm.
"Aha, my little dear" I say,
"your clan will pay me back one day."

— *Dorothy Parker*

✛

Most men lead lives of quiet desperation and
go to the grave with the song still in them.

— *Henry David Thoreau*

Living is death; dying is life. We are not what we appear to be. On this side of the grave we are exiles, on that citizens; on this side orphans, on that children.

— *Henry Ward Beecher*

✝

I have seen a thousand graves opened, and always perceived that whatever was gone, the teeth and hair remained of those who had died with them. Is not this odd? They go the very first things in youth and yet last the longest in the dust.

— *Lord Byron*

Babies haven't any hair;
Old men's heads are just as bare;
Between the cradle and the grave
Lie a haircut and a shave.

— Samuel Hoffenstein

✛

Life was a funny thing that happened to me
on the way to the grave.

— Quentin Crisp

If after all that we have lived and thought,
All comes to Nought,—
If there be nothing after Now,
And we be nothing anyhow,
And we know that,—why live?

— *Edwin Arlington Robinson*

✠

There is little much beyond the grave, but
the strong are saying nothing until they see.

— *Robert Frost*

Let us so live that when we come to die even the undertaker will be sorry.

— *Mark Twain*

✠

Done with the work of breathing; done
With all the world; the mad race run
Through to the end; the golden goal
Attained and found to be a hole!

— *Ambrose Bierce*

It is a modest creed, and yet
Pleasant if one considers it,
To own that death itself must be,
Like all the rest, a mockery.

— *Percy Bysshe Shelley*

✦

It's impossible to experience one's death
objectively and still carry a tune.

— *Woody Allen*

✦

Dying is easy, comedy is hard.

— *Edmund Gwenn (asked on his deathbed whether
dying is hard)*

We are American at puberty. We die French.

— Evelyn Waugh

✠

In Europe they have taken half the
cigarette packet to tell you smoking kills. I'm
going to insist it should also say on the back,
"Death awaits you whether you smoke or not."

— David Hockney

✠

The paths of glory lead but to the grave.

— Thomas Gray

In the long run we are all dead.

— John Maynard Keynes

✠

Don't you find it a beautiful, clean thought,
a world empty of people, just uninterrupted
grass, and a hare sitting up?

— D. H. Lawrence

✠

All that has achieved existence deserves to
be destroyed.

— Goethe

The world begins and ends with us. Only our consciousness exists, it is everything, and this everything vanishes with it.

— *E. M. Cioran*

✛

Either this man is dead or my watch has stopped.

— *Groucho Marx*

Our current obsession with creativity is the result of our continued striving for immortality in an era when most people no longer believe in an afterlife.

—Arianna Huffington

✠

Ancient Egyptians believed that upon death they would be asked two questions and their answers would determine whether they could continue their journey in the afterlife. The first question was, "Did you bring joy?" The second was, "Did you find joy?"

—Leo Buscaglia

I am ready to meet my Maker. Whether my Maker is prepared for the great ordeal of meeting me is another matter.

— *Winston Churchill*

✝

Man is so muddled, so dependent on the things immediately before his eyes, that every day even the most submissive believer can be seen to risk the torments of the afterlife for the smallest pleasure.

— *Joseph de Maistre*

A belief in hell and the knowledge that
every ambition is doomed to frustration
at the hands of a skeleton have never
prevented the majority of human beings
from behaving as though death were no
more than an unfounded rumor.

— Aldous Huxley

✠

Believing in hell must distort every
judgment on this life.

— Cyril Connolly

When I think of the number of disagreeable people that I know who have gone to a better world, I am sure hell won't be so bad at all.

— Mark Twain

To work hard, to live hard, to die hard, and then go to hell after all would be too damned hard.

— Carl Sandburg

The supreme satisfaction is to be able to despise one's neighbor and this fact goes far to account for religious intolerance. It is evidently consoling to reflect that the people next door are headed for hell.

— Aleister Crowley

I believe that I am in hell, therefore I am there.

— Arthur Rimbaud

Between us and heaven or hell there is only life, which is the frailest thing in the world.

— Blaise Pascal

✝

The safest road to hell is the gradual one—the gentle slope, soft underfoot, without sudden turnings, without milestones, without signposts.

— C. S. Lewis

Here there is no hope, and consequently no duty, no work, nothing to be gained by praying, nothing to be lost by doing what you like. Hell, in short, is a place where you have nothing to do but amuse yourself.

— *George Bernard Shaw*

✣

Hell is paved with great granite blocks hewn from the hearts of those who said, "I can do no other."

— *Heywood Broun*

So this is hell. I'd never have believed it. You remember all we were told about the torture chambers, the fire and brimstone, the "burning marl." Old wives' tales! There's no need for red-hot pokers. Hell is other people.

— *Jean-Paul Sartre*

✢

Those who promise us paradise on earth never produced anything but a hell.

— *Karl Popper*

Hell is where no one has anything in common with anybody else except the fact that they all hate one another and cannot get away from one another and from themselves.

— *Thomas Merton*

✠

Hell is a city much like London.

— *Percy Bysshe Shelley*

For mortal men there is but one hell, and
that is the folly and wickedness and spite of
his fellows; but once his life is over, there's
an end to it: his annihilation is final and
entire, of him nothing survives.

— Marquis de Sade

✝

Let me go to hell, that's all I ask, and go on
cursing them there, and them look down
and hear me, that might take some of the
shine off their bliss.

— Samuel Beckett

We must prefer real hell to an imaginary
paradise.

— *Simone Weil*

Hell is oneself, hell is alone, the other
figures in it merely projections. There is
nothing to escape from and nothing to
escape to. One is always alone.

— *T. S. Eliot*

The infliction of cruelty with a good conscience is a delight to moralists. That is why they invented hell.

— Bertrand Russell

✝

The philosopher is Nature's pilot. And there you have our difference: to be in hell is to drift: to be in heaven is to steer.

— George Bernard Shaw

✝

An intelligent hell would be better than a stupid paradise.

— Victor Hugo

I desire to go to hell and not to heaven. In the former place I shall enjoy the company of popes, kings, and princes, while in the latter are only beggars, monks, and apostles.

— *Niccolò Machiavelli*

✛

Maybe this world is another planet's hell.

— *Aldous Huxley*

✛

Parting is all we know of heaven and all we need of hell.

— *Emily Dickinson*

Men have feverishly conceived a heaven only to find it insipid, and a hell to find it ridiculous.

— George Santayana

✠

How well I have learned that there is no fence to sit on between heaven and hell. There is a deep, wide gulf, a chasm, and in that chasm is no place for any man.

— Johnny Cash

If the destination is heaven, why do we scramble to be first in line for hell?

— *Doug Horton*

✠

The mind is its own place, and in itself can make heaven of hell, a hell of heaven.

— *John Milton*

✠

It is a statistical fact that the wicked work harder to reach hell than the righteous do to enter heaven.

— *Josh Billings*

I don't like to commit myself about heaven
and hell; you see, I have friends in both
places.

— *Mark Twain*

✢

I would rather go to heaven alone than go to
hell in company.

— *R. A. Torrey*

✢

Heaven for climate, Hell for company.

— *James M. Barrie*

Heaven, *n*. A place where the wicked cease from troubling you with talk of their personal affairs and the good listen with attention while you expound your own.

—*Ambrose Bierce*

✠

Heaven: the Coney Island of the Christian imagination.

—*Elbert Hubbard*

The human mind is inspired enough when it comes to inventing horrors; it is when it tries to invent a heaven that it shows itself cloddish.

— *Evelyn Waugh*

☩

Heaven, as conventionally conceived, is a place so inane, so dull, so useless, so miserable, that nobody has ever ventured to describe a whole day in heaven, though plenty of people have described a day at the seaside.

— *George Bernard Shaw*

Heaven goes by favor; if it went by merit, you would stay out and your dog would go in.

— *Mark Twain*

✣

It is a curious thing . . . that every creed promises a paradise which will be absolutely uninhabitable for anyone of civilized taste.

— *Evelyn Waugh*

As the fly bangs against the window attempting freedom while the door stands open, so we bang against death ignoring heaven.

— *Doug Horton*

✠

This world is the land of the dying; the next is the land of the living.

— *Tyron Edwards*

We were born to die and we die to live. As seedlings of God, we barely blossom on earth; we fully flower in heaven.

— *Russell M. Nelson*

✝

There is not much sense in suffering, since drugs can be given for pain, itching, and other discomforts. The belief has long died that suffering here on earth will be rewarded in heaven. Suffering has lost its meaning.

— *Elisabeth Kübler-Ross*

Men long for an afterlife in which there apparently is nothing to do but delight in heaven's wonders.

— Louis D. Brandeis

✦

I do not believe in an afterlife, although I am bringing a change of underwear.

— Woody Allen

✦

Of all the inventions of man I doubt whether any was more easily accomplished than that of a heaven.

— Georg C. Lichtenberg

If you go to heaven without being naturally qualified for it, you will not enjoy yourself there.

— George Bernard Shaw

✠

You forget that the kingdom of heaven suffers violence: and the kingdom of heaven is like a woman.

— James Joyce

I find the great thing in this world is not so much where we stand, as in what direction we are moving: To reach the port of heaven, we must sail sometimes with the wind and sometimes against it, but we must sail, and not drift, nor lie at anchor.

— Oliver Wendell Holmes

✠

Some people are so heavenly minded that they are no earthly good.

— Oliver Wendell Holmes

A lawyer's dream of heaven: every man reclaimed his property at the resurrection, and each tried to recover it from all his forefathers.

— Samuel Butler

✛

The bottom line is in heaven.

— Edwin H. Land

✛

In heaven all the interesting people are missing.

— Nietzsche

God is the big question mark. Heaven is the even bigger question mark. Death is just another question mark.

— *Emmylou Harris*

✝

Everybody wants to go to heaven, but nobody wants to die.

— *Joe Louis*

Index

A—C

Ace, Goodman 21
Adam, Juliette 127
Ade, George 112
Aeschylus 118
Alcott, Louisa May 75
Allen, Woody 5, 10, 38, 79, 86, 112, 133, 158
Allston, John 45
American proverb 96
Amis, Kingsley 76
Angelou, Maya 110
Anonymous 26, 30, 55, 60
Arnauld, Antoine 53
Asimov, Isaac 4, 74
Auden, W. H. 3, 16
Augustine, Saint 101
Aurelius, Marcus 122
Bacon, Francis 32
Bankhead, Tallulah 50
Barrie, James M. 152
Barry, Dave 77
Baudelaire, Charles 11
Baudrillard, Jean 54
Becker, Ernest 27, 71
Beckett, Samuel 146

Beecher, Henry Ward 129
Behrman, S. N. 37
Benét, Stephen Vincent 79
Benny, Jack 116
Berger, John 16
Berra, Yogi 113
Betjeman, John 78
Bhagavad Gita 119
Bierce, Ambrose 91, 92, 93, 98, 102, 132, 153
Billings, Josh 151
Bishop, Jim 3
Blythe, Ronald 7
Bolt, Robert 118
Borges, Jorge Luis 43
Boucicault, Dion 51
Brandeis, Louis D. 158
Brecht, Bertolt 118
Brooks, Mel 78
Broun, Heywood 44, 80, 143
Brown, Rita Mae 30
Buddha 61, 70
Bujold, Lois McMaster 99
Burchill, Julie 105
Burgess, Anthony 24
Burns, George 35
Burr, Amelia 69
Burroughs, William S. 59
Buscaglia, Leo 137
Butler, Nicolas 95
Butler, Samuel 40, 99, 161
Byrnes, James F. 75

Byron, Lord 129
Caen, Herb 38
Camus, Albert 31
Canetti, Elias 22
Carlin, George 13
Carlyle, Thomas 2, 126
Carson, Johnny 121
Cary, Joyce 80
Cash, Johnny 150
Cather, Willa 66
Céline, Louis-Ferdinand 13
Chamfort, Nicolas 86
Chandler, Steve 56
Chesterton, G. K. 28
Church, F. Forrester 72
Churchill, Winston 60, 138
Cioran, E. M. 136
Cobb, Irvin S. 95, 101
Cocteau, Jean 32
Cohen, M. R. 32
Colton, Charles Caleb 102
Comte, Auguste 126
Connolly, Cyril 97, 139
Cousins, Norman 81
Crisp, Quentin 130
Crowley, Aleister 141

D–F

Darrow, Clarence 58
Defoe, Daniel 8
de Gaulle, Charles 46
de Maistre, Joseph 138
de Saint-Exupéry, Antoine 19

de Unamuno, Miguel 82
Dickinson, Emily 31, 37, 149
Donne, John 35
Dylan, Bob 119
Eddy, Mary Baker 67
Edwards, Tyron 156
Einstein, Albert 34, 90
Elfman, Danny 36
Eliot, George 109
Eliot, T. S. 147
Emerson, Ralph Waldo 69, 104
Epicurus 120
Ertz, Susan 42
Euripedes 83
Feynman, Richard 12
Fitzgerald, Edward 31
Flecker, James Elroy 36
Forster, E. M. 106
Franklin, Benjamin 55, 62
Freud, Sigmund 1, 49
Frewer, Matt 122
Frohman, Charles 62
Fromm, Erich 29
Frost, Robert 96, 100, 131
Fuller, R. Buckminster 95
Furnas, J. J. 2

G–J

Gauguin, Paul 52
Genesis 3:19 1
Gibran, Kahlil 56, 65
Gilman, Charlotte Perkins 70
Goethe 52, 135

Goldwyn, Samuel 124
Gray, Thomas 134
Gwenn, Edmund 133
Hall, Bishop 4
Hammerstein, Oscar II 33
Harris, Emmylou 162
Harris, Mark 22
Hawthorne, Nathaniel 65
Hazlitt, William 5
Heine, Heinrich 14, 41
Heller, Joseph 42, 79
Hendrix, Jimi 14
Hepburn, Katharine 124
Hoagland, Edward 39
Hoban, Russell 6
Hockney, David 134
Hoffenstein, Samuel 130
Hoffer, Eric 34, 83
Holmes, Oliver Wendell 30, 160
Hope, James Barron 83
Horace 21
Horton, Doug 151, 156
Housman, A. E. 115
Howe, Ed 59
Hubbard, Elbert 2, 153
Huffington, Arianna 137
Hugo, Victor 148
Huxley, Aldous 8, 139, 149
Ingalls, John J. 21
Ingersoll, Robert G. 67
Ionesco, Eugene 17

J—L

Johnson, Samuel 88
Joplin, Janis 15
Joyce, James 159
Jung, Carl 27
Kaufman, George S. 44, 93
Keleman, Stanley 48
Keynes, John Maynard 135
King, Martin Luther, Jr. 57
Kübler-Ross, Elisabeth 4, 7, 28, 157
La Bruyère 98
Land, Edwin H. 161
Larkin, Philip 63
Latin saying 127
Lawrence, D. H. 135
Lec, Stanislaw J. 37
Leonardo da Vinci 81, 121
Lerner, Max 77
Levenson, Sam 116
Lewis, C. S. 142
Lichtenberg, Georg C. 158
Longfellow, Henry Wadsworth 74
Louis, Joe 162
Lyon, Clare Harner 92

M—O

Machiavelli, Niccolò 149
Macmillan, Harold 111
Malraux, André 5, 82
Mann, Thomas 84
Mansfield, Katherine 10
Manson, Charles 6
Marshall, Arthur 113

Martial 100
Marvell, Andrew 9
Marx, Groucho 136
Maugham, W. Somerset 124, 127
Meltzer, David 84
Mencken, H. L. 23, 26
Mendelssohn, Moses 41
Merton, Thomas 145
Millay, Edna St. Vincent 72
Miller, Jonathan 25
Milton, John 53, 151
Mitchell, Margaret 55
Mitford, Jessica 110
Mitford, William 85
Mizner, Wilson 125
Morris, Robert T. 103
Munroe, H. H. 58
Murdoch, Iris 87
Nabokov, Vladimir 26
Nelson, Russell M. 157
Nietzsche 43, 161
Nin, Anaïs 84
Nordau, Max 40
Nuland, Sherwin B. 25, 47
Nunn, Gregory 99
Ogden, Howard 11
O'Rourke, P. J. 107
Orwell, George 85

P–R

Parker, Dorothy 17, 48, 128
Pascal, Blaise 142
Pavese, Cesare 65
Péguy, Charles 14
Penn, William 52
Phillips, John 66
Pike, Albert 40
Plato 1
Popper, Karl 144
Porter, Katherine Anne 15
Publilius Syrus 20, 33
Radner, Gilda 73
Raymond, Rossiter W. 61
Richter, Jean Paul 18
Rimbaud, Arthur 141
Rinpoche, Sogyal 76
Robinson, Edwin Arlington 131
Roman epitaph 94
Russell, Bertrand 148

S–V

Sachs, A. 117
Sade, Marquis de 146
Sahl, Mort 113
Salinger, J. D. 91
Sandburg, Carl 140
Santayana, George 121, 150
Saroyan, William 24
Sartre, Jean-Paul 24, 144
Schnitzler, Arthur 22
Schwartz, Morrie 20

Scott, Sir Walter 64
Segal, Erich 101
Seneca 57, 86, 87
Shakes, Ronnie 115
Shakespeare, William v, 53
Shaw, George Bernard 45, 104, 120, 125, 143, 148, 154, 159
Shelley, Percy Bysshe 133, 145
Simenon, Georges 33
Simpsons, The 11
Singer, Isaac Bashevis 3
Smith, Logan Pearsall 18
Smith, Red 23
Socrates 13, 64, 66
Sophocles 123
Spark, Muriel 17
Stalin, Joseph 47
Stoppard, Tom 54
Stowe, Harriet Beecher 108
Tacitus, Publius Cornelius 44
Tagore, Rabindranath 57
Taylor, John 18
Thomas, Dylan 63
Thomas, Gwyn 111
Thoreau, Henry David 51, 128
Thornton, Billy Bob 116
Thurber, James 38, 89
Tolstoy, Leo 12
Tomlin, Lily 10
Torrey, R. A. 152
Truth, Sojourner 89

Twain, Mark 8, 46, 50, 58, 89, 90, 97, 103, 108, 132, 140, 152, 155
Van Dyke, Henry 85
Vidal, Gore 9
Voltaire 109, 126
Vonnegut, Kurt 117
Wallace, William 61
Waugh, Evelyn 134, 154, 155
Weil, Simone 147
Wheelis, Allan 92
Whitman, Walt 62
Whittier, John Greenleaf 114
Wilcox, Ella Wheeler 114
Wilde, Oscar 105, 122
Williams, Tennessee 29, 49
Wittgenstein, Ludwig 39, 68
Woodman, Marion 68
Woolf, Virginia 20
Yeats, William Butler 51
Yee, Rodney 123
Yiddish proverb 23, 50
Yogananda, Paramhansa 67
Young, Brigham 64
Yourcenar, Marguerite 88
Zapata, Emiliano 115
Zen saying 12

About the Author

Jon Winokur lives in
Pacific Palisades, California.
Temporarily.